ST. LOUIS
CARDINALS TRIVIA

Mike Getz

Quinlan Press
Boston

Copyright © 1987
by Mike Getz
All rights reserved,
including the right of reproduction
in whole or in part in any form.
Published by Quinlan Press
131 Beverly Street
Boston, MA 02114

ISBN 1-55770-026-5

Cover design by Lawrence Curcio

Printed in the United States of America
November 1987

Mike Getz, a freelance writer, has been an ardent sports fan for over forty years. His contributions have appeared in a number of magazines and newspapers, including *Baseball Digest, Baseball Bulletin* and *Diamond Report*. As a member of the Society for American Baseball Research, Getz was one of the chief organizers of the first annual New York SABR Regional held at Shea Stadium in 1984. His previous books include *Baseball's 3,000-Hit Men, New York Yankees Trivia* and *New York Mets Trivia*. His many radio appearances include "The Art Rust Show" (WABC) and "In the Public Interest" (WHN). Mr. Getz lives with his wife, Virginia, and teenage son, Vincent, in Brooklyn, New York.

A special thanks to John Grabowski for his encouragement and for providing much-needed research materials; to Scott Flatow, baseball's number-one trivia expert; and to Vincent Getz for typing and editing much of this manuscript.

TABLE OF CONTENTS

HISTORY
Questions........................ 1
Answers......................... 11
WORLD SERIES
Questions........................ 19
Answers......................... 31
AT THE PLATE AND ON THE BASES
Questions........................ 39
Answers......................... 49
THE BATTERY
Questions........................ 57
Answers......................... 73
PHOTOGRAPHS
Questions........................ 85
Answers......................... 97
INFIELD
Questions........................ 99
Answers......................... 109
OUTFIELD
Questions........................ 117
Answers......................... 123
MANAGERS AND COACHES
Questions........................ 129
Answers......................... 135
MISCELLANEOUS
Questions........................ 139
Answers......................... 151

History

1. How old was Tim McCarver when he got his first major league hit?

2. What team was the only one to come back after trailing in a game, 11-0?

3. Who were Cardinal teammates for six years, had the same last name, but were not related?

4. In what year did every Cardinal regular bat over .300?

5. On October 7, 1969, what outfielder tested baseball's reserve clause by refusing to report when traded to the Phillies?

History—Questions

6. What players were swapped in the Cards-Phillies deal involving Curt Flood?

7. During a Cardinals-Cubs doubleheader, what players switched teams?

8. Who was the first Cardinal to win the Rookie of the Year award?

9. How many consecutive games did Stan Musial play?

10. What teams were the first to play in a major league game outside the U.S.?

11. When were the Cardinals officially given their name?

12. When did the team first occupy Sportsman's Park?

13. What teams played in the first Sunday game in NL history?

14. What was Stan Musial's biggest consecutive-game hitting streak?

15. Bob Forsch pitched no-hitters against what two teams?

16. In what year was Jim Bottomley most valuable?

History—Questions

17. Which three Cardinals won MVP Awards during the 1960s?

18. Which three Cardinals won MVP Awards during the 1930s?

19. During the 1940s, St. Louis Cardinal players won MVP Awards three straight years. Name them.

20. When did the Cards play their first night game in St. Louis?

21. In what year did the Cardinals reach the one-million mark in attendance for the first time?

22. In what year did the Cards reach the two-million mark in attendance for the first time?

23. In what years did Stan Musial win Most Valuable Player awards?

24. For what pennant-winning team did Showboat Fisher bat .374?

25. On September 17, 1968, Gaylord Perry of the Giants pitched a no-hitter against the Cards. On the next day, what Cardinal pitched a no-hitter against the Giants?

26. In 1944 what 15-year-old pitcher made his major league debut against the Cardinals in an 18-0 Card victory?

3

History—Questions

27. Who pulled an unassisted triple play against the Cardinals?

28. When did the Cardinals win their first World Series and whom did they beat?

29. When did Busch Memorial Stadium open?

30. What Cardinal pitcher won the first game in the new Busch Stadium?

31. Who got the first Cardinal hit in Busch Stadium?

32. Who hit the first home run in the new stadium?

33. In 1968 how many earned runs did Bob Gibson allow in 304 innings pitched?

34. What career milestones did Joe Torre reach while with the Cardinals in 1973?

35. In 1975 who finished second to BIll Madlock in NL batting?

36. Who shared MVP honors with Keith Hernandez in 1979?

37. Name the first switch-hitter to get 100 hits both left and righthanded in one season?

History—Questions

38. What players were involved in the Lou Brock trade?

39. What Hall-of-Fame pitcher was traded by the Cardinals after his rookie season and went on to win 20 games for six straight years?

40. Who did the Cardinals get when they traded Steve Carlton?

41. Who was traded to the Redbirds for the 1985 stretch run and batted .434 (33-76)?

42. Name the player who led the 1934 Gashouse Gang in homers, RBIs, batting, slugging, hits, runs and total bases.

43. When the Cardinals won it all in 1931, how many players hit 20 home runs and how many had 100 RBIs?

44. When did the Cardinals get shut out twice in a doubleheader that lasted 27 innings?

45. When did Rogers Hornsby win the Triple Crown?

46. Who was the last NL player to win the Triple Crown?

47. When Rogers Hornsby was traded for Frankie Frisch (December 20, 1926), who else did the Cardinals get?

5

History—Questions

48. When did the Cardinals use a yellow baseball?

49. Who was the only player in major league history to hit a yellow baseball for a home run?

50. What teams played a 25-inning night game?

51. Who scored the winning run in the above game for the Cards?

52. What did Dizzy Dean do on the day brother Paul pitched a no-hitter?

53. When Hornsby set an NL record for homers in 1922, who gave up the final two homers?

54. Who scored the winning run for the NL in the bottom of the tenth inning for a 2-1 victory in the 1966 All-Star Game?

55. When did the Cardinals score ten runs in one inning twice in one game?

56. When St. Louis came back into the National League in 1892, where did they finish in the standings?

57. In what seasons did the Cardinals finish twelfth, and what was the team's record?

History—Questions

58. How many games did the 1943 Cardinals win the flag by?

59. When did St. Louis play St. Louis in the World Series?

60. Who was the last National Leaguer to bat over .370?

61. How close was the 1964 pennant race?

62. What was the Cardinals' won-lost record for the last 51 games of 1942?

63. Whose pitching career ended abruptly in the spring of 1941 when he hurt his shoulder in training camp?

64. Whom did Stan Musial beat out for MVP in 1943?

65. Whom did Mort Cooper beat out for MVP in 1942?

66. Name the two Cardinal players who had three hits each in the first playoff game in NL history (1946)?

67. In 1982 what Cardinal favorite pitched a three-hit shutout against Atlanta in the opening game of the NLCS?

68. What rookie tripled and homered in the pennant-clinching game against Atlanta in 1982?

History—Questions

69. Whose three-run ninth-inning homer won the 1985 pennant for the Cardinals?

70. Which Cardinal was selected World Series MVP in 1982?

71. How many home runs did the pennant-winning Cardinals hit in 1982?

72. Who was the first Cardinal to have his uniform number retired?

73. What two Cardinals had 150-RBI seasons?

74. When was the last time a Cardinal led the league in home runs?

75. What teams participated in the major league's first season-opening night game?

76. Which was the only team since 1900 to lose the first four games of the season and win the pennant?

77. Name the two Cardinals who won MVP awards in their first seasons with the team after being traded away by another club.

78. Whom did the Cardinals trade for Willie McGee?

79. Whom did the Cardinals trade to get Jack Clark?

History—Questions

80. Who was traded with catcher Mike Heath to the Cards for pitcher Joaquin Andujar (December 10, 1985)?

81. Whom did the Cardinals get when they traded Ken Reitz to the Giants?

82. What Cardinal third baseman was traded for two MVPs?

83. What Cardinal pitcher was traded for two MVPs?

84. Name the three switch-hitters on the Gashouse Gang.

85. What was the score of the game in which Jim Bottomley went 6-for-6 and drove in 12 runs?

86. Name the first player to bat in a major league game in Canada.

87. Who hit the major league's first grand slam in Canada?

88. What team was the first to lose in Canada?

89. In a swap of future Hall-of-Famers, whom did the Cardinals get when they traded Burleigh Grimes to the Cubs?

90. What was the Cardinals team batting average in 1930?

History—Questions

91. What is the highest total of runs scored by the Cardinals in a single game?

92. Where did the Cardinals finish in 1965—the year after they won the World Series?

93. Where did the Cardinals finish in 1966—the year before they won the World Series?

94. What was the closest three-way race for the batting crown?

95. In 1918 the Cardinals led the league in home runs. Where did they finish that year?

96. Who gave up the first home run (to Babe Ruth) in All-Star Game history?

97. Who hit the first pinch-hit grand slam in major league history?

98. When did the Cardinals play their first home night game; what was the result?

99. What was the last wooden ballpark in the majors?

100. Which team had a better record—the 1943 or 1944 Cardinals?

Answers

1. Seventeen

2. The Cardinals trailed the N. Y. Giants, 11-0, on June 15, 1952, and rallied to win, 14-12.

3. Del and Hal Rice

4. 1930

5. Curt Flood

6. The Cards replaced Flood (who refused to report) with Willie Montanez and Bob Browning. Also going to the Phillies were Tim McCarver, Joe Hoerner and Byron

History—Answers

Browne. The Redbirds acquired Richie Allen, Cookie Rojas and Jerry Johnson.

7. On May 30, 1922, between games of a doubleheader, the Cards traded outfielder Cliff Heathcote to the Cubs for outfielder Max Flack.

8. Wally Moon (1954)

9. 895

10. The Cardinals played the Expos in Montreal on April 14, 1969.

11. In 1899

12. In 1920

13. The Reds defeated the Cards on Sunday, April 17, 1892.

14. Thirty games in 1950

15. The Phillies (1978) and the Expos (1983)

16. 1928

17. Ken Boyer (1964), Orlando Cepeda (1967) and Bob Gibson (1968)

18. Frankie Frisch (1931), Dizzy Dean (1934) and Joe Medwick (1937)

History—Answers

19. Mort Cooper (1942), Stan Musial (1943) and Marty Marion (1944)

20. In 1940

21. 1946

22. 1967

23. 1943, 1946 and 1948

24. The 1930 Cardinals

25. Ray Washburn

26. Joe Nuxhall of the Reds

27. Pirate shortstop Glenn Wright (May 7, 1925)

28. 1926, the Yankees

29. May 12, 1966

30. Don Dennis

31. Mike Shannon

32. Mike Shannon

33. Only 38

34. 2,000 hits and 1,000 RBIs

History—Answers

35. Ted Simmons hit .332

36. Willie Stargell of the Pirates

37. Garry Templeton

38. The Cubs traded Brock with pitchers Jack Spring and Paul Toth to the Cardinals for pitchers Ernie Broglio and Bobby Shantz and outfielder Doug Clemens.

39. Mordecai (Three-finger) Brown

40. Pitcher Rick Wise

41. Cesar Cedeno

42. First baseman Ripper Collins

43. None

44. On July 2, 1933, the Cards lost a twin bill to the Giants by identical scores of 1-0. The first game went 18 innings.

45. 1922 and 1925

46. Joe Medwick (1937)

47. Pitcher Jimmy Ring

48. On August 2, 1938, the Cardinals and Dodgers used a yellow baseball in a game in Brooklyn.

History—Answers

49. Johnny Mize

50. The Cards beat the Mets, 4-3, at Shea Stadium on September 11, 1974.

51. Bake McBride

52. In a double-header with Brooklyn, Dizzy Dean pitched a three-hit shutout prior to brother Paul's no-hitter (September 21, 1934).

53. Home run number 41 was hit off Jesse Barnes of the Giants and number 42 off his brother Virgil Barnes.

54. Tim McCarver

55. On July 6, 1929, the Cards had two 10-run innings en route to a 28-7 victory over the Phillies.

56. Eleventh (56-94)

57. 1897 (29-102) and 1898 (39-111)

58. Eighteen

59. 1944

60. Stan Musial hit .376 in 1948

61. The Cardinals won the pennant by one game over both the Phillies and the Reds and by three games over the Giants.

History—Answers

62. The Cards won 43 and lost 8

63. Stan Musial

64. Teammate Walker Cooper (catcher)

65. Teammate Enos Slaughter

66. Terry Moore and Joe Garagiola (October 1, 1946)

67. Bob Forsch

68. Willie McGee

69. Jack Clark

70. Darrell Porter

71. 67, a major league low

72. Stan Musial—number 6

73. Medwick (154) and Hornsby (152)

74. 1940 (Johnny Mize hit 43.)

75. The Cardinals beat the Pirates, 4-2, on April 18, 1950.

76. The 1985 Cardinals

77. Bob O'Farrell (1926) acquired from the Cubs, and Orlando Cepeda (1967) acquired from the Giants.

History—Answers

78. Pitcher Bob Sykes

79. Pitcher Dave LaPoint, infielder Jose Uribe and first basemen/outfielders David Green and Gary Rajsich.

80. Pitcher Tim Conroy

81. Pitcher Pete Falcone

82. Charley Smith was traded to the Cards for Ken Boyer and traded by the Cards for Roger Maris.

83. Ray Sadecki was traded by the Cards for Orlando Cepeda and re-acquired by the Cards for Joe Torre.

84. Ripper Collins, Frankie Frisch and Jack Rothrock

85. Cardinals 17, Brooklyn 3

86. Lou Brock (April 14, 1969 in Montreal)

87. Dal Maxvill (against the Expos, April 14, 1969)

88. The Cardinals

89. Hack Wilson and pitcher Bud Teachout

90. .314

History—Answers

91. 28—against the Phillies on July 6, 1929

92. Seventh

93. Sixth

94. In 1931 Chick Hafey of the Cardinals batted .3489, Bill Terry of the Giants batted .3486, and Jim Bottomley of the Cardinals batted .3482.

95. Last!

96. Wild Bill Hallahan

97. Mike O'Neill (1902)

98. June 4, 1940—Dodgers 10, Cards 1.

99. Robison Field was the home of the Cardinals until July 6, 1920.

100. Both clubs had a 105-49 record.

World Series

1. What Rookie of the Year pitched in three World Series games the year before he won the award?

2. Who celebrated his birthday while playing in the 1982 World Series?

3. Name the only Cardinal to hit safely in all seven World Series games in 1985.

4. Name the only player to steal three bases in a World Series game—twice.

5. Which World Series record was tied by both Harry Brecheen and Bob Gibson?

6. How did rookie Joe Garagiola hit in the 1946 World Series?

World Series—Questions

7. What Hall-of-Famer pitched a two-hitter and drove in the winning runs in Game Three to put the Cards ahead in the 1931 Series?

8. Name the pitcher who lost two games in the 1930 World Series and won two games in the Series the following year?

9. What pitcher was the top winner in the league in 1931 and won two additional games for the Cards in the World Series?

10. What Cardinal teams won the World Series without even one 20-game winner?

11. What Cardinal has the highest lifetime batting average in World Series history?

12. Who batted only 26 times during the regular season (1964), but batted 20 times in the World Series that year?

13. Who had no hits in 22 at-bats in the 1968 Series?

14. Who played in all seven games of the 1964 World Series and batted .478?

15. How many Tiger hitters did Bob Gibson strike out when he set a World Series record in Game One of the 1968 Series?

World Series—Questions

16. Who hit three homers in a World Series game against the Cardinals—twice?

17. Who pitched and won the final game of the 1934 World Series and what was the score of the game?

18. He came in from the bullpen in the seventh inning of the seventh game of the 1926 World Series and struck out Tony Lazzeri of the Yankees with the bases loaded. Name him.

19. True or false? Tiger pitcher Denny McLain beat the Cards three times in the 1968 World Series.

20. What was the opening-game score of the 1982 World Series between the Cardinals and Milwaukee Brewers?

21. What Milwaukee player set a World Series record by getting five hits in the 1982 opener against the Cardinals?

22. What pitcher started four World Series games for the Cards and lost all four?

23. Who tied Eddie Collins record by stealing 14 bases in World Series competition?

24. Who was the victim of Stan Musial's only World Series homer?

21

World Series—Questions

25. What Cardinal pitcher gave up the home run to Mickey Mantle that broke Babe Ruth's World Series record?

26. What pitcher retired the last 21 Yankee batters in a row to win Game Two of the 1926 World Series?

27. With two out in the ninth of the seventh game of the 1926 World Series, who ended the Series by getting thrown out trying to steal second base?

28. Whom did the Cardinals walk 11 times in the 1926 Series?

29. In 1926 what light-hitting Cardinal shortstop led all hitters with a .417 World Series average?

30. Whose three-run homer in the seventh inning won Game Two of the 1926 World Series?

31. How many times have the Cardinals and Yankees met in the World Series?

32. What Yankee slugger hit four home runs in four games against the Cardinals in the 1928 World Series?

33. Whose two-run homer in the ninth inning broke up a 0-0 World Series game and enabled the Philadelphia A's to beat the Cards?

World Series—Questions

34. What Hall-of-Fame Cardinal outfielder hit five doubles during a World Series?

35. After five games in the 1931 World Series who had 12 hits in 18 at-bats (.667)?

36. Who led the World Champion Cardinals in batting, slugging, runs, hits, doubles and stolen bases in the 1931 World Series?

37. In the 1931 Series, what player scored all the Cards' runs in Game Two, had all the Cards' hits in Game Four, and drove in all but one of the Cards' runs in Game Five?

38. What Cardinal pitcher tossed shutouts in both the 1930 and 1931 World Series?

39. What Cardinal pitcher pinch-ran in the World Series, failed to slide going into second base, and was nailed on the head by a throw to first?

40. Who was taken out in the middle of the last game of the 1934 World Series (by the baseball commissioner) for his own protection?

41. Name the Tiger third baseman that Joe Medwick slid hard into (with the Cards

23

World Series—Questions

ahead 9-0) setting off a near riot in the last game of the 1934 Series.

42. True or false? The Dean brothers won all four World Series games in 1934.

43. In the 1934 World Series, the Cardinals faced a Tiger lineup with three Hall-of-Famers whose last names begin with G. Name them.

44. What Cardinal pitcher knocked in the winning run in Game Six of the 1934 Series and tied the Series at three games apiece?

45. Whose great throw in Game Two of the 1942 Series cut down the tying run at third with none out in the ninth?

46. Who won only seven games all season but shut-out the Yanks in the 1942 World Series?

47. Who homered in the ninth inning to give the Cardinals their fourth victory in the 1942 Series?

48. What was unusual about the schedule for the 1943 World Series?

49. What was unusual about the schedule for the 1944 World Series?

World Series—Questions

50. Who struck out the first five batters he faced in Game Five of the 1943 World Series?

51. Which Cardinal ace pitched a two-hitter to open the 1944 World Series (against the Browns) but lost the game?

52. Whose pinch-hit single drove in the winning run in the bottom of the eleventh to even the 1944 Series (1-1)?

53. Name the rookie manager who led the Cardinals to the world championship in 1946.

54. Who homered in the tenth inning to beat the Cards in the opening game of the 1946 World Series?

55. What three Cardinals had four hits each in Game Four of the above World Series?

56. In Game Seven of the 1946 Series, Enos Slaughter kept running from first base and scored the winning run on whose hit?

57. True or false? Howie Pollet won three games in the 1946 World Series.

58. True or false? In the 1946 World Series Enos Slaughter scored from first base on a single.

25

World Series—Questions

59. Whose grand slam accounted for all the runs in a 4-3 World Series victory over the Yankees?

60. Whose three-run homer in the tenth inning gave the Cardinals a three-games-to-two edge in the 1964 World Series?

61. Who managed the Cardinals to the world championship in 1964?

62. Name the Red Sox pitcher who one-hit the Cardinals in the 1967 World Series?

63. Who got the only Cardinal hit in the above game?

64. In the 1967 Series, what Cardinal homered with two out in the ninth to spoil Jim Lonborg's bit for his second straight shutout?

65. How many batters did Bob Gibson walk and strike out during the 1967 Series?

66. Who batted 840 times in his career but hit his only home run in the 1968 World Series against the Cardinals?

67. How many consecutive games did Bob Gibson win in World Series play?

68. Who threw Lou Brock out at the plate in the 1968 World Series?

World Series—Questions

69. What rookie pitcher started two games for the Cardinals in the 1982 World Series?

70. What former Cardinal homered against the Cards in the first and second games of the 1982 World Series?

71. Who had two four-hit games for the Brewers against the Cards in the 1982 fall classic?

72. Who was surprisingly the leading batter for the Cards in the 1944 Series?

73. How many RBIs did Roger Maris get in the 1967 World Series?

74. When Bob Gibson struck out his 32nd batter in the 1968 Series, whose record did he break?

75. What rookie outfielder hit two home runs and made two great catches in the same World Series game in the 1982 Series?

76. What Cardinal set a record with nine hits as a DH in the World Series?

77. What two World Series ended in seven games with the final game score 11-0?

78. What Cardinal pitcher gave up World Series homers to Carl Yastrzemski, Reggie Smith and Rico Petrocelli—in the same inning?

World Series—Questions

79. Name the only major leaguer to get four hits in a World Series game and four hits in an All-Star Game?

80. Who missed the 1985 World Series when his leg got caught from behind in the tarpaulin?

81. Who replaced Vince Coleman in the 1985 Series and batted .360?

82. In the 1982 World Series, what Cardinal drove in two runs on one sacrifice fly?

83. In which Cardinal World Series did the batting champions meet?

84. Name the only brothers to hit home runs in the same World Series game.

85. What two players hit World Series homers for both the Cards and the Yanks?

86. Who played the most games in World Series history without hitting a homer?

87. Who hit homers in the 1967 and 1968 World Series but hit no homers during the regular 1967 and 1968 seasons?

88. Name the leftfielder who replaced Joe Medwick in the last game of the 1934 World Series.

World Series—Questions

89. Who stole home in the 1964 World Series?

90. How many times have the Cards won the World Series by taking the seventh game?

91. Have the Cardinals ever been swept in the World Series?

92. How many games have the Cardinals and Yankees played against each other in the World Series?

93. Name the first designated hitter to get three extra-base hits in a World Series game (1982)?

Answers

1. Todd Worrell

2. Keith Hernandez

3. Tito Landrum (9-25, .360)

4. Lou Brock (1967, 1968)

5. They each won three games in one World Series.

6. Garagiola got six hits (including two doubles) in 19 at-bats and drove in four runs for a .316 average.

7. Burleigh Grimes

World Series—Answers

8. Burleigh Grimes

9. Bill Hallahan

10. The 1931 and 1967 Cardinals

11. Pepper Martin (23-for-55, .418)

12. Dal Maxvill

13. Card shortstop Dal Maxvill

14. Tim McCarver (11-for-23)

15. Seventeen

16. Babe Ruth in 1926 and 1928

17. Dizzy Dean blanked the Tigers, 11-0

18. Grover Cleveland Alexander

19. False; it was Mickey Lolich.

20. The Brewers beat the Cardinals, 10-0

21. Paul Molitor

22. Bill Sherdel lost two games in 1926 and two more in 1928

23. Lou Brock

World Series—Answers

24. Sig Jackucki of the Browns (1944)

25. Barney Schultz

26. Grover Alexander

27. Babe Ruth

28. Babe Ruth

29. Tommy Thevenow

30. Billy Southworth

31. Five: the Cards won in 1926, 1942 and 1964. The Yanks won in 1928 and 1943.

32. Lou Gehrig

33. Jimmie Foxx (1930)

34. Chick Hafey (1930)

35. Pepper Martin

36. Pepper Martin

37. Pepper Martin

38. Bill Hallahan

39. Dizzy Dean

World Series—Answers

40.   Leftfielder Joe Medwick

41.   Marv Owen

42.   True

43.   Goose Goslin, Hank Greenberg and Charlie Gehringer

44.   Paul Dean

45.   Enos Slaughter

46.   Ernie White

47.   Whitey Kurowski

48.   Due to wartime travel restrictions the first three games were played at Yankee Stadium with the remaining four to be played in St. Louis.

49.   There were no travel days in between games as all games were played in the same stadium (Sportsman's Park — home of both the Cards and Browns).

50.   Mort Cooper (against the Yankees)

51.   Mort Cooper

52.   Ken O'Dea

World Series—Answers

53. Eddie Dyer

54. Rudy York (Red Sox)

55. Enos Slaughter, Whitey Kurowski and Joe Garagiola

56. Harry Walker

57. False — it was Harry (The Cat) Brecheen.

58. False

59. Ken Boyer

60. Tim McCarver

61. Johnny Keane

62. Jim Lonborg

63. Julian Javier

64. Roger Maris

65. Gibby walked five and struck out 26.

66. Pitcher Mickey Lolich

67. Seven

68. Willie Horton

World Series—Answers

69. John Stuper

70. Ted Simmons

71. Robin Yount

72. Emil (The Antelope) Verban batted .412 (7-for-17).

73. Seven

74. His own Series record of 31, set in 1964

75. Willie McGee

76. Dane Iorg

77. 1934 (Cards won) and 1985 (Cards lost)

78. Dick Hughes (1967)

79. Joe Medwick (WS-1934) (ASG-1937)

80. Vince Coleman

81. Tito Landrum

82. Tommy Herr flied to Brewers centerfielder Gorman Thomas who stumbled after the catch. Both Willie McGee and Ozzie Smith tagged up and scored after the catch.

World Series—Answers

83. 1931 (Cards Chick Hafey and Philadelphia A's Al Simmons)

84. Ken and Clete Boyer (1964)

85. Enos Slaughter and Roger Maris

86. Frankie Frisch played 50 World Series games and batted 197 times with no homers.

87. Bob Gibson

88. Chick Fullis

89. Tim McCarver

90. Seven — 1926, 1931, 1934, 1946, 1964, 1967 and 1982.

91. Yes: in 1928 the Cards lost four straight to the Yanks.

92. Although the Cards won three World Series out of five from the Yanks, in games played the Yanks lead 15-13.

93. Dane Iorg

At the Plate
and on the Bases

1. Which Cardinal once drove in 12 runs in a nine-inning game?

2. Who batted safely in 19 straight games for the 1987 Cardinals?

3. What was Ken Boyer's biggest consecutive-game hitting streak?

4. Who hit safely in 28 straight games for the 1954 Cards?

5. What are the most home runs Stan Musial hit in one afternoon?

6. Whose single-season stolen base record did Lou Brock break?

At the Plate and on the Bases—Questions

7. Who broke Brock's stolen base record?

8. How many consecutive seasons did Lou Brock steal 50 or more bases?

9. How close did Brock come to stealing 1,000 bases?

10. What Cardinal had one hit in his career — a home run?

11. What Cardinal had the highest total in lifetime homers without having led the league?

12. How many times did Stan Musial hit 40 or more homers?

13. What Cardinal pitchers stole home?

14. What Cardinal pitcher stole 13 bases during his career?

15. How many of Lou Brock's 938 stolen bases were steals of home?

16. Who batted .465 (20-for-43) as a pinch-hitter for the 1938 Cards?

17. How many consecutive seasons did Jim Bottomley get at least 30 doubles and 10 triples?

At the Plate and on the Bases—Questions

18. Who smacked his 100th career pinch hit while playing for the Cardinals in 1984?

19. What was Stan Musial's 3,001st hit?

20. During his career, did Stan Musial get more hits at home or on the road?

21. From Lou Brock's first season with the Cards (1964), to his record-breaking stolen base season (1974), what was his average number of hits per season?

22. Who spend two seasons with the Cardinals, nine years apart, and was the NL's top pinch-hitter in 1971?

23. Who was the team runner-up in RBIs to league-leader Cepeda in 1967?

24. Prior to 1987, what was Jack Clark's best RBI year?

25. How many bases did Vince Coleman steal in his first full season at Macon?

26. Who pinch-hit safely 24 times for the Cardinals in 1970?

27. What former Mets manager was the best pinch-hitter in the National League as a Cardinal in 1954?

41

At the Plate and on the Bases—Questions

28. What Cardinal reserve just missed batting .400 (33-for-83) for the 1977 season but failed to hit .250 the next season?

29. Whose 50-year-old record for most hits by a switch-hitter in one season was broken by Pete Rose?

30. What Cardinal set a record by hitting three home runs in his first two major league games?

31. Who was the first player to get a pinch-hit homer in his first major league at-bat?

32. What other Cardinal homered in his first at-bat (1954)?

33. How many triples, homers and stolen bases did Keith Hernandez get in his MVP year?

34. In the early fifties who played three positions for the Cards and led the NL in pinch-hits two years in a row?

35. In 1987 who was the only player in the NL with over 400 at-bats and no home runs?

36. Who was the only catcher in NL history to lead the league in triples?

At the Plate and on the Bases—Questions

37. What Gashouse Gang member averaged 50 doubles per year during a six-year period in his career?

38. In what three categories did Willie McGee lead when he won the MVP Award in 1985?

39. Johnny Bench hit three straight homers off what Cardinal pitcher?

40. Who was the only player in NL history to hit over 50 home runs in one season and bat over .360 in another?

41. Who was the last National Leaguer to score *and* drive in 135 or more runs in the same season?

42. How many times did Stan Musial bat over .350?

43. Who hit the first NL homer in All-Star Game history?

44. In the 1948 All-Star Game who homered with a man on in the top of the first inning for the only two runs for the National League?

45. Name the Cardinal who won the All-Star Game in 1950 with a 14th-inning home run.

At the Plate and on the Bases—Questions

46. In how many All-Star Games did Stan Musial homer?

47. Who gave up the 12th-inning, game-winning home run to Stan Musial in the 1955 All-Star Game?

48. Against what team did Lou Brock steal his 893d base — the one that broke Ty Cobb's lifetime record?

49. What Cub pitcher gave up Lou Brock's 3,000th hit?

50. In what city did Stan Musial get his 3,000th hit?

51. What pitcher gave up Stan Musial's 3,000th hit?

52. What Cardinal was league runner-up to Hornsby during two of his batting championship seasons?

53. When Medwick won the triple crown in 1937, what Cardinal was second in NL batting with a .364 average?

54. Before Willie Mays reached 20 doubles, triples and homers in 1957, who was the last National Leaguer to go 20-20-20?

55. In 1936 what rookie led the Cards in homers, drove in 93 runs and batted .329?

At the Plate and on the Bases—Questions

56. How were Joe Medwick's batting totals amazingly similar in 1935 and 1936?

57. In 1939 what three Redbirds socked 144 doubles among them?

58. How old was Stan Musial when he first led the league in hits (220), doubles (48), triples (20), batting (.375) and slugging (.562)?

59. In 1946 who led the National League in hits by a margin of 44?

60. Stan Musial batted .300 or more for how many consecutive seasons?

61. In what years did the Cardinals steal 314 bases — fourth highest in baseball history?

62. Who stole more bases in one season than any Cardinal first baseman?

63. In what years did Cardinal teams steal 200 or more bases for six straight seasons?

64. Name the five Cardinals who stole 30 or more bases in 1985.

65. As a Cardinal, who hit more doubles, Rogers Hornsby or Enos Slaughter?

66. How many times did Stan Musial lead the league in doubles?

45

At the Plate and on the Bases—Questions

67. True or false? Other than Stan Musial, no one hit over 200 homers as a Cardinal.

68. What was the difference in the number of runs Stan Musial scored and the number of runs he drove in (lifetime)?

69. Which four active players are among the top eight Cardinal base-stealers lifetime?

70. After 1920, in what decade did no Cardinal win a batting title?

71. Prior to Jack Clark, who was the last Cardinal to hit 30 home runs in one season?

72. What is the Cardinals' team record for homers in one season?

73. Prior to 1987, who was the last Cardinal to lead the league in RBIs?

74. Prior to his lone season with the Cardinals (1981), who hit grand-slams on opening-day games — twice?

75. Who broke Hornsby's National League record (set in 1922) for most homers in one season (42)?

76. What Cardinal batted three times as an All-Star and got three hits?

At the Plate and on the Bases—Questions

77. What Cardinals homered in the All-Star Game and in the World Series the same year?

78. What Dodger hurler gave up Jack Clark's pennant-winning homer in 1985?

79. Where and when did Lou Brock break Maury Wills's stolen base record?

80. Who pinch-ran for Stan Musial in his final at-bat?

81. Who gave up Pete Rose's 3,631st hit — the one that broke Musial's NL record?

82. Name the two Cardinals to get five doubles in one day.

83. In 1970 which Cardinal struck out five straight times in one game?

84. How many times was Ron Hunt hit by a pitch?

85. Name the only Cardinal to steal five bases in one game.

86. During his career, how many times was Lou Brock caught stealing?

87. True or false? The Cardinals once left 24 men on base in one game.

At the Plate and on the Bases—Questions

88. Name the player who holds the career record for home runs by a National League switch-hitter.

89. During his career, how many times did Frankie Frisch steal home?

90. Name the last pitcher to get a hit in an All-Star Game.

91. In 1934 whose double ruined future Cardinal Lon Warneke's bid for a no-hitter?

92. As a team, what did the Cardinals bat against Atlanta in the NLCS in 1982?

93. Who holds the major league record for most hits in one season by a catcher?

94. What St. Louis Cardinal was caught stealing 36 times in one season?

95. Name the first switch-hitters on the same team to drive in 100 or more runs.

Answers

1. Jim Bottomley (September 16, 1924)

2. Terry Pendleton

3. 29 games in 1959

4. Red Schoendienst

5. Five — in a doubleheader against the Giants

6. Maury Wills

7. Rickey Henderson

8. Twelve

At the Plate and on the Bases—Answers

9. Brock missed by 62 bases. He stole 938 times.

10. Ron Allen

11. Stan Musial — 475

12. None

13. Curt Simmons stole the plate as a result of a missed squeeze play. Back in 1913, Slim Sallee also stole home.

14. Bob Gibson

15. None

16. Frenchy Bordagaray

17. For seven straight years (nine altogether) Bottomley had 30 doubles and 10 triples.

18. Steve Braun

19. A home run

20. Musial got 1,815 hits at home and 1,815 hits on the road.

21. During those 11 seasons, Brock averaged 194 hits.

22. Bob Burda

At the Plate and on the Bases—Answers

23. Mike Shannon drove in 77 runs.

24. Clark drove in 103 with San Francisco in 1982.

25. 145

26. Vic Davalillo

27. Joe Frazier (20-for-62)

28. Roger Freed

29. Frankie Frisch got 223 hits in 1923 (as a Giant).

30. Joe Cunningham (June 30 and July 1, 1954).

31. Eddie Morgan (1936) — it was the only home run in his career.

32. Wally Moon

33. 11 triples, 11 homers, 11 stolen bases

34. "Peanuts" Lowery

35. Ozzie Smith

36. Tim McCarver led the NL with 13 three-baggers in 1966.

At the Plate and on the Bases—Answers

37.   Joe Medwick

38.   Batting (.353), hits (216) and triples (18)

39.   Steve Carlton

40.   Johnny Mize

41.   Johnny Mize

42.   Five

43.   Frankie Frisch

44.   Stan Musial

45.   Red Schoendienst

46.   Six

47.   Boston Red Sox' Frank Sullivan

48.   San Diego Padres

49.   Dennis Lamp

50.   Chicago

51.   Moe Drabowsky of the Cubs

52.   Jim Bottomley batted .371 in 1923 and .367 in 1925, second to Hornsby for the batting crown — twice!

At the Plate and on the Bases—Answers

53.   Johnny Mize

54.   Jim Bottomley in 1928 (42 doubles, 20 triples, 31 home runs)

55.   Johnny Mize

56.
	Games	AB	HITS	BA	SLG
1935-	154	634	224	.353	.576
1936-	155	636	223	.351	.577

57.   Slaughter (52), Medwick (48) and Mize (44) finished first, second and third in the National League in doubles.

58.   Twenty-two

59.   Stan Musial had 228 hits; runner-up Dixie Walker had 184.

60.   Seventeen

61.   1985

62.   Jack Fournier stole 26 in 1920

63.   Cardinal teams from 1982 to 1987 stole 200 or more bases each year.

64.   Coleman 110, McGee 56, Van Slyke 34, Herr 31 and Ozzie Smith 31

65.   Hornsby 367, Slaughter 366

At the Plate and on the Bases—Answers

66. Eight times

67. False — Ken Boyer hit 255 homers as a Cardinal (282 overall).

68. Two! 1,949 scored; 1,951 RBIs.

69. Coleman, McGee, Lonnie Smith and Ozzie Smith

70. The sixties

71. Dick Allen belted 34 in 1970.

72. 143 in 1955

73. Joe Torre (137 in 1971)

74. Sixto Lezcano

75. Chuck Klein (43) in 1929

76. Tim McCarver

77. Joe Medwick (1934) and Ken Boyer (1964)

78. Tom Niedenfuer

79. In Philadelphia on September 10, 1974

80. Gary Kolb

At the Plate and on the Bases—Answers

81. The Cardinals' Mark Littell (August 10, 1981)

82. Joe Medwick and Red Schoendienst (in doubleheaders)

83. Dick Allen

84. 243

85. Lonnie Smith (September 4, 1982)

86. 307

87. True — in a 17-inning game against the Pirates

88. Ted Simmons had 176 NL homers going into the 1987 season.

89. Nineteen times

90. Steve Carlton (1969)

91. Ripper Collins

92. .330

93. Ted Simmons (193 in 1975)

94. Miller Huggins

95. Ted Simmons (103) and Reggie Smith (100) in 1974

The Battery

1. What newly acquired Cardinal regular broke his left thumb in the third game of the 1987 season?

2. What Cardinal catcher had two 19-game hitting streaks during his career?

3. Who are the only brothers to pitch major league no-hitters?

4. How many years did Cardinal catcher Bob O'Farrell play big-league baseball?

5. When did Bob Gibson win the Cy Young Award?

6. Since 1900, who was the first Cardinal to throw a no-hitter?

The Battery—Questions

7. From 1935 to 1967, who was the only Cardinal to toss a no-hitter?

8. Who struck out 19 batters in a game but lost the ballgame?

9. Who was Bob Gibson's 3,000th strikeout victim?

10. What Cardinal pitcher gave up Henry Aaron's first home run?

11. Who was a 21-game winner for the Cardinals at age 40?

12. In the past 40 years, who was the only Cardinal pitcher other than Bob Gibson to win 20 games two years in a row?

13. Who had an amazing won-lost record of 29-11 while with the Cardinals?

14. Name the lefty starter and reliever who had nine winning seasons in ten years — all spent with the Cardinals.

15. In the 1940s, who won 15 out of 18 decisions coming out of the bullpen?

16. Who was known as "The Cat"?

17. What Cardinal pitcher was called "The Kitten"?

The Battery—Questions

18. In what pitching categories did Harry Brecheen lead the league in 1948?

19. What pre-1900 Cardinal hurler accomplished the following within a two year period: started 100 games, completed 92 games, won 45 and lost 55?

20. Who was the top winner for the 1967 world champs?

21. Who was the main man out of the bullpen for the 1968 NL champs?

22. Who pitched for at least 31 pro baseball teams (nine major league), finishing his big-league career with the Cardinals?

23. How many games did Steve Carlton win in his last season with the Cardinals?

24. Who pitched for the Cards in 1952 and 1953 and retired with a perfect 3-0 record?

25. What native Canadian won 40 games for the Cardinals between 1971 and 1973?

26. How many times did Mort Cooper pitch a shutout from 1942 to 1944?

27. Where was pitcher Danny Cox born?

The Battery—Questions

28. What was Dizzy Dean's real name?

29. Who won more games in his first two full seasons — Dizzy or Paul Dean?

30. Who was the last NL pitcher to win 30 games in one season?

31. Name the rookie pitching star for the 1931 Redbirds.

32. Which two Cardinals hurlers led the league in earned run average twice?

33. Who had by far the best season of his career, getting 21 wins as a Cardinal, although he played for another team until late May?

34. Name the Cardinal pitcher who lost 33 games in one season.

35. Prior to 1900, what 300-game winner finished his career with the Cardinals?

36. How many times was Bob Gibson a 20-game winner?

37. In what pitching category did Bob Gibson most frequently lead the league?

38. What St. Louis catcher went from the Cards to the Giants to the Cards to the Cubs to the Cards?

The Battery—Questions

39. Who lost exactly five games for the Red-birds for three straight years and had a 34-17 record with the club during the forties?

40. In 1957 what 18-year-old St. Louis rookie pitched a brilliant two-hit, 2-0 win over the Dodgers in his first start?

41. In 25 total decisions for 1974 and 1975, what was Al Hrabosky's won-lost record?

42. The Cardinals have had three pitchers named Jackson. Give their first names.

43. In 1980 who pitched an extra-inning shutout for St. Louis at age 41?

44. What member of the 1979 and 1980 Cards once pitched in all seven games of a World Series?

45. Prior to his final season, who complied an amazing 37-9 lifetime pitching record?

46. What Cardinal pitcher won 13 of his first 14 major league decisions?

47. What Card hurler had a perfect 10-0 record in 1941?

48. What former Cardinal catcher is the son of a 16-year American Leaguer?

61

The Battery—Questions

49. What veteran catcher spent 14 years with the Reds, Cubs, Giants, Mets, Orioles, Senators and Cardinals?

50. In 1954 what rookie pitcher went 15-6 for a sixth-place Cardinal team?

.51 What five Cardinal pitchers (names beginning with "L") are listed one after another in the Baseball Encyclopedia with no other players in between?

52. What brothers pitched on the 1911 and 1912 Cardinals?

53. What reserve catcher batted .366 (83 hits) for the 1930 pennant winners?

54. Name the Hall-of-Fame pitcher who beat the Cardinals by pitching an 18-inning shutout and walking nobody.

55. Between 1959 and 1980, what year did Tim McCarver not play in the major leagues?

56. Who is first on the all-time list for games won in relief?

57. Before Lindy McDaniel went 12 straight years without starting a game, what was his best season as a starter?

The Battery—Questions

58. What Cardinal pitchers were named after presidents?

59. Over 100 years ago, who pitched the first Cardinal no-hitter?

60. What Cardinal pitcher was once a 41-year-old NL rookie?

61. What pitcher started his career with the Redbirds but also pitched for the Mets, Dodgers, Cubs, Padres, Pirates, Twins, Indians, White Sox and Tigers?

62. Who pitched one season with the Cardinals (1958) and finished his career with a 10-1 lifetime record?

63. How many times in his career did Dizzy Dean have a losing season?

64. Name the popular catcher who caught 11 years with the Cards during the forties and fifties and continued to catch until 1961.

65. When did the city of St. Louis have one brother catching for the Cardinals while another brother caught for the Browns?

66. How old was Carl Scheib when he completed his 11-year major league career?

67. What three-game Cardinal pitched for ten teams in only nine years.

63

The Battery—Questions

68. In 1901 Cardinal catcher Pop Schriver led the NL in pinch-hits with how many?

69. What Cardinal hurler had his biggest winning season in his 17th major league campaign?

70. What Cardinal pitcher set a National League record by saving 45 games in 1984?

71. Name the Cardinal hurler whose first and last names were the same.

72. How old was Hall-of-Fame pitcher Dazzy Vance when he was traded to the Cardinals?

73. Name the rookie pitcher who broke in with a 17-4 record in 1944.

74. How many consecutive years did Cy Young win 20 games or more?

75. What rookie pitcher posted an 11-1 record in relief (12-2 overall) for the 1952 Cards — and never won or lost another big-league game?

76. Prior to 1900, who pitched 16 shutouts in one season for the Cards?

77. Name the pitcher who in 1876 won and lost all 64 Cardinal games?

The Battery—Questions

78. Who was the starting pitcher for the National League in the 1942 and 1943 All-Star Games? .

79. What Hall-of-Famer was nicknamed "Ol' Stubblebeard"?

80. How old was "Pop" Haines when he won his last game for the Cards?

81. True or false? Dizzy and Paul Dean pitched for the St. Louis Browns.

82. What Cardinal pitcher once played for the Harlem Globetrotters?

83. At age 26, what Hall-of-Fame pitcher fractured his toe in an All-Star Game and was never quite the same?

84. Who was the star pitcher for the 1926 world champs?

85. What was Hall-of-Famer Grover Alexander's nickname?

86. Who had 20-game winning seasons for the Phillies and Cubs before he was a 20-game winner for the Cards?

87. Name the two .300-hitting catchers who shared the backstopping duties for the 1930 pennant winners.

The Battery—Questions

88. How many times did Dizzy Dean strike out 200 batters in a season?

89. Just how good was the Cardinal pitching staff in 1943?

90. Name the rookie pitcher and future umpire who had a 19-8 record for the 1945 Cards.

91. In 1949 who pitched in more games, won more games in relief and saved more games than anyone in the league?

92. How many times has Bruce Sutter led the league in saves?

93. How many consecutive games did Bob Gibson win in 1968?

94. How many times did John Tudor pitch a shutout in 1985?

95. In 1985 what Cub spoiled Tudor's bid for a no-hitter?

96. Who wore uniform number 13 for the Cards in the early forties?

97. Out of 24 ballots, how many first place votes did Todd Worrell get for Rookie of the Year?

The Battery—Questions

98. How many games did Dizzy Dean predict he and his brother Paul would win for the 1934 Cards? How many did they actually win?

99. What uniform number did Bob Gibson wear?

100. Other than Bob Gibson, what Cardinal pitcher struck out over 200 batters in one season while leading the league?

101. Name the only Cardinal pitcher to lead the league in ERA and also pitch a no-hitter.

102. What Card pitcher lost 50 games with the team but won over 100?

103. What Card pitcher drove in the most runs in one season?

104. In 1911 who started 41 games on the mound for the Cardinals — a club record that stands over 75 years later?

105. Who started 286 games during his career and completed every game but eight?

106. In 1968 how many games did Bob Gibson win by a 1-0 score?

107. In 1953 who had an 18-9 record for the Cards while hitting 17 batters?

67

The Battery—Questions

108. What future Hall-of-Famer lost the first game ever at the new Busch Stadium?

109. How many times did Bob Gibson pitch the first game of the season for the Cardinals?

110. What pitcher gave up only two grand slams in 15 major league seasons — both to Steve Garvey?

111. Name the only brothers to start as pitcher and catcher in the All-Star Game.

112. What Cardinal pitcher gave up the first run in All-Star Game history?

113. How many no-hitters has Steve Carlton thrown?

114. What New York Giant pitcher threw a five-inning no-hitter against the Cardinals in his major league debut?

115. Name the only Cardinal to reach base in Cub Don Cardwell's no-hitter.

116. Before Don Cardwell no-hit the Cards, how long had it been since anyone no-hit the Redbirds?

117. Whose last victory was a no-hitter before being traded to the Cardinals?

68

The Battery—Questions

118. Who played the parts of Dizzy and Paul Dean in the movie *Pride of St. Louis?*

119. Who portrayed Grover Cleveland Alexander in the movie *The Winning Team?*

120. How many times did Bob Gibson lead the league in strikeouts?

121. What Cardinal was a 21-game winner in his 17th major league season?

122. Who was called "Spittin' Bill"?

123. Who were the Cardinals' pitcher and catcher at the moment Maury Wills broke Ty Cobb's stolen base record?

124. On September 15, 1969, in a game against the Mets, who was Steve Carlton's record-breaking 19th strikeout victim?

125. When Gibson fanned a record 17 Tigers in a World Series game, who was his 17th victim?

126. Name the losing pitcher in Gaylord Perry's 1-0 no-hitter against the Cards on September 17, 1968.

127. Which Cardinal was the losing pitcher in back-to-back All-Star Games?

69

The Battery—Questions

128. What Cardinal lefty shut out the Los Angeles Dodgers five times in one season?

129. Who struck out Cardinal Walter Alston in his only big-league at-bat?

130. Who was the first National League pitcher to win an All-Star Game?

131. How old was Von McDaniel when he played his last major league game?

132. What Cardinal pitcher lost the first major league game played in Canada?

133. Name the last Cardinal pitcher to throw a legal spitball.

134. Name the pitcher who surrendered Stan Musial's final hit.

135. Who was the last batter to get a hit off Bob Gibson?

136. For what major league team did Curt Simmons pitch last?

137. What Cardinal hurler came from Egypt, Pennsylvania?

138. Who led the league in shutouts in 1966 by pitching all his shutouts against the same team?

70

The Battery—Questions

139. What Cub batter did Stan Musial pitch to in a game on September 28, 1952?

140. What Cardinal pitcher gave up Ernie Banks's first major league home run?

141. In 1908 the Cardinals won 49 and lost 105. How many times were they shut out that year?

142. Who pitched the first no-hitter against the Cardinals in 41 years?

143. Prior to 1960, who was last to no-hit the Cardinals?

144. Who pitched 352 innings in one season for the Cards and never needed relief?

145. What former Cardinal reliever has a degree in engineering as well as one in medicine?

146. What Cardinal relief pitcher was born the day of Don Larsen's perfect game?

147. What Card pitcher was the victim of 11 shutouts in one season?

148. In 1924 what ironman feat did rookie pitcher Hi Bell accomplish that has not been achieved in the last 63 years?

The Battery—Questions

149. Who pitched two one-hitters and two two-hitters among his nine wins in 1978?

150. Since 1900, who walked more batters than any pitcher in National League history?

151. Name the pitcher and catcher who formed the first brother battery in modern baseball.

152. Of pitcher Steve Carlton's 14 opening-day assignments, how many were with St. Louis?

153. What was the score of Grover Alexander's 373d and final victory?

154. In the 1981 split season, who was the Cardinals' starting pitcher on both opening days?

155. What Cardinal pitcher won his final ten major league decisions?

156. Although Tom Seaver won the baseball writers award for Rookie of the Year in 1967, who did the *Sporting News* pick for Rookie Pitcher of the Year?

157. What stopped Howie Pollet's consecutive-scoreless-inning streak at 28?

Answers

1. Catcher Tony Pena

2. Ted Simmons (1973 and 1975)

3. Bob and Ken Forsch

4. Twenty-one

5. 1968 and 1970

6. Jesse "Pop" Haines (1924)

7. Lon Warneke (1941, at Cincinnati)

8. Steve Carlton fanned 19 batters but lost, 4-3, to the Mets (September 15, 1969).

The Battery—Answers

9. Cesar Geronimo of the Reds (July 17, 1974)

10. Vic Raschi

11. Grover Cleveland Alexander

12. Joaquin Andujar won 20 in 1984 and 21 in 1985.

13. Johnny Beazley

14. Alpha Brazle

15. Alpha Brazle

16. Pitcher Harry Brecheen

17. Harvey Haddix

18. Brecheen led the NL in percentage (20-7, .741), ERA (2.24), strikeouts (149) and shutouts (7).

19. Ted Breitenstein

20. Dick Hughes (16-6)

21. Joe Hoerner (8-2, 17 saves, 1.47 ERA)

22. George Brunet

23. Twenty in 1971

The Battery—Answers

24. Mike Clark

25. Reggie Cleveland

26. Cooper pitched 23 shutouts from 1942 to 1944.

27. Northampton, England

28. Jay Hanna Dean

29. Neither — each Dean totaled 38 wins in his first two seasons.

30. Dizzy Dean (30-7 in 1934)

31. Paul Derringer (18-8, .692)

32. Bill Doak in 1914 and 1921 and Howie Pollet in 1943 and 1946

33. Red Barrett

34. Red Donahue (11-33 in 1897)

35. Pud Galvin (361-310)

36. Five times

37. Gibson led in shutouts four times

38. Mike Gonzalez

The Battery—Answers

39. Harry Gumbert

40. Von McDaniel

41. Hrabosky won 21 and lost 4 in that two-year period.

42. Al, Larry and Mike

43. Jim Kaat

44. Darold Knowles (1973, with the Oakland A's)

45. Howie Krist

46. Howie Krist

47. Howie Krist

48. Terry Kennedy (Father Bob Kennedy played from 1939 to 1957.)

49. Hobie Landrith

50. Brooks Lawrence

51. Littell, Little, D. Littlefield, J. Littlefield and Littlejohn

52. Grover and Lou Lowdermilk

53. Gus Mancuso

The Battery—Answers

54. Carl Hubbell

55. 1962

56. Hoyt Wilhelm (123)

57. In 1957 L. McDaniel was 15-9 with ten complete games.

58. U.S. Grant McGlynn, George Washington Bradley and Grover Cleveland Alexander

59. George Bradley on July 15, 1876, against Hartford

60. Diomedes Olivo

61. Bob Miller

62. Phil Paine

63. None

64. Del Rice

65. In 1927 Bobby Schang caught three games for the Cards. His brother Wally caught for the St. Louis Browns.

66. Twenty-seven

67. Dick Littlefield

The Battery—Answers

68. Three

69. Curt Simmons started his major league career in 1947. His biggest win total was 18 in 1964.

70. Bruce Sutter

71. Thomas Thomas

72. Forty-two

73. Ted Wilks

74. Young was a 20-game winner for 14 straight years.

75. Eddie Yuhas

76. George Bradley

77. George Bradley

78. Mort Cooper

79. Pitcher Burleigh Grimes

80. Forty-four

81. True — Paul pitched three games in 1943; Dizzy started once in 1947.

82. Bob Gibson

The Battery—Answers

83. Dizzy Dean

84. Flint Rhem (20-7)

85. "Pete"

86. Grover Alexander

87. Jim Wilson and Gus Mancuso

88. None; but Dean struck out over 190 four times

89. The Cardinals' pitching staff led the NL in strikeouts and all major league clubs in shutouts (21), ERA (2.57) and complete games (94). Seven pitchers won at least twice as many games as they lost.

90. Ken Burkhart

91. Ted Wilks

92. Five Times

93. Fifteen

94. Ten

95. Leon Durham

96. Mort Cooper

The Battery—Answers

97. Twenty-three

98. Dean predicted 50; the Deans won 49 between them.

99. Number 45

100. Sam Jones fanned 225 in 1958

101. Bob Gibson has a 1.12 ERA in 1968 and pitched a no-hitter in 1971.

102. Mort Cooper

103. Dizzy Dean drove in 21 runs in 1935

104. Bob Harmon

105. Jack Taylor

106. Four

107. Gerry Staley

108. Phil Niekro

109. Ten

110. Clay Carroll

111. Mort and Walker Cooper

112. Wild Bill Hallahan

The Battery—Answers

113. None

114. Red Ames

115. Alex Grammas

116. Forty-one years

117. Cliff Chambers (1951 Pirates)

118. Dan Dailey played Dizzy; Richard Crenna played Paul.

119. Ronald Reagan

120. Once

121. Grover Alexander

122. Cardinal pitcher and two-time 20-game winner Bill Doak

123. Pitcher Larry Jackson; catcher Carl Sawatski

124. Amos Otis

125. Willie Horton

126. Bob Gibson

127. Mort Cooper

The Battery—Answers

128. Larry Jaster

129. Lon Warneke of the Cubs

130. Dizzy Dean (1936)

131. Nineteen

132. Gary Waslewski

133. Burleigh Grimes in 1934

134. Jim Maloney of the Reds

135. Pete LaCock of the Cubs

136. California Angels (1967)

137. Curt Simmons

138. Larry Jaster

139. Frankie Baumholtz

140. Gerry Staley (September 20, 1953)

141. Thirty-three times

142. Don Cardwell of the Cubs (May 16, 1960)

143. Hod Eller of the Reds (May 11, 1919)

144. Jack Taylor (1904)

The Battery—Answers

145. Ron Taylor

146. Jeff Lahti (October 8, 1956)

147. Bugs Raymond (1908)

148. Bell pitched two complete-game victories in one day

149. Silvio Martinez

150. Steve Carlton walked 1,717 batters while pitching in the NL

151. Pitcher Mike O'Neill and catcher Jack O'Neill (1902)

152. One

153. 19-16, Cards beat the Phillies

154. Bob Forsch

155. Eddie Yuhas

156. Dick Hughes (16-6)

157. He entered military service

Photographs

1. Identify this player standing with Stan Musial.

Photographs—Questions

The St. Louis Cardinals

2. In 1968 how many of Bob Gibson's 22 wins were shutouts?

Photographs—Questions

3. How many times did Orlando Cepeda bat over .300?

Photographs—Questions

4. In the 1967 World Series Roger Maris led all players in what category?

Photographs—Questions

5. How many consecutive years did Lou Brock steal 35 or more bases?

Photographs—Questions

The St. Louis Cardinals

6. Name this famous portrait artist.

Photographs—Questions

The St. Louis Cardinals

7. What was Red Schoendienst's best batting mark?

Photographs—Questions

The St. Louis Cardinals

8. What is Dal Maxvill's given name?

Photographs—Questions

9. What award did Ozzie Smith win *during* the 1985 season?

Photographs—Questions

10. How old was Jack Clark when he got his first major league hit?

Photographs—Questions

The St. Louis Cardinals

11. Including 1987, how many seasons had Bob Forsch pitched for the Cardinals?

Photographs—Questions

12. How many triples did Tim McCarver get when he led the league in 1966?

Answers

1. Shortstop Daryl Spencer

2. Thirteen

3. Nine

4. RBIs—seven

5. Fourteen years in a row

6. Curt Flood

7. Red batted .342 in 1953.

8. Charles Dallan Maxvill

9. The MVP of the NLCS

Photographs—Answers

10. Nineteen

11. Fourteen

12. Thirteen

The Infield

1. Who was the only major leaguer to get 14 hits within two days?

2. In the 1950s, what Cardinal infielder broke in with two 100-RBI seasons and was then traded?

3. Who was the only Cardinal to hit into an unassisted triple play?

4. Who hit a grand-slam homer when two Mets outfielders collided trying to catch the ball?

5. Who had the highest batting average for Hornsby's 1926 Cards?

The Infield—Questions

6.   Who was called "The Blazer"?

7.   How tall was Gashouse Gang first base-
        man Ripper Collins?

8.   What Redbird was second to Hank
        Aaron's .355 for the 1959 batting crown?

9.   What Russian-born Cardinal was up for
        a "cup of coffee" (three games) in 1921?

10.   Who was the .300-hitting regular short-
        stop for the 1930 NL champs?

11.   What NL infielder more than doubled his
        RBI total from 1984 to 1985?

12.   Other than Ken Boyer, what Card third
        baseman had two brothers in the majors?

13.   What Cardinal Hall-of-Famer played in
        four different cities in four years?

14.   Who batted .360 or higher for four dif-
        ferent major league teams?

15.   How many batting championships did
        Rogers Hornsby win?

16.   From 1960 to 1971, who was the Car-
        dinals' steady second-sacker?

17.   Who was born on the day Babe Ruth
        died?

The Infield—Questions

18. Name the Cardinal third baseman who hit 27 home runs and drove in 104 runs in 1947.

19. What was "Rabbit" Maranville's real name?

20. What Hall-of-Famer played shortstop for the Braves, Pirates, Cubs, Dodgers and Cardinals?

21. What defensive great was known as "Slats"?

22. In what category did Red Schoendienst lead the league in his rookie season?

23. What 39-year-old was the National League's best pinch-hitter in 1962?

24. From 1977 to 1979, what Cardinal hit 50 triples in three years and led the league for three straight years?

25. In what categories did Joe Torre lead the league in his MVP year (1971)?

26. What Cardinal infielder of the 1970s has the same name as a heavyweight boxing champion?

27. How many years did Bobby Wallace play big-league ball?

The Infield—Questions

28. In the early sixties what Cardinal batted over .300 while driving in 100 or more runs for three straight years?

29. Who got three hits and made three great fielding plays for the National League in the 1956 All-Star Game?

30. Who holds the club one-season record for highest fielding percentage by a second baseman?

31. Who tied a record with four doubles in the NLCS against the Dodgers in 1985?

32. When did Ozzie Smith win his first Gold Glove Award?

33. Who set a major league record for short-stops with 621 assists in one season?

34. Who set a major league record for second baseman with 641 assists in one season?

35. What was Rogers Hornsby's major position in his first full season?

36. Who was the regular shortstop for the 1926 world champs?

37. In what fielding categories did Marty Marion most frequently lead NL short-stops?

The Infield—Questions

38. How many times did second baseman Red Schoendienst have the best fielding percentage in the National League?

39. Who led NL third basemen in fielding in 1973, 1974, 1977, 1978 and 1980?

40. Who was the Cardinals' leading vote-getter for MVP in 1941?

41. Who did Frankie Frisch call "the best team player in the National League"?

42. Who did Connie Mack call "the greatest shortstop I have ever seen"?

43. What three Cardinals pulled off two triple plays within two weeks?

44. What five-year Card infielder (1938-1942) broke his leg while playing in the Army and never played major league ball again?

45. From what team did the Cards acquire Jose Oquendo?

46. What Cardinal third baseman had a league-leading 46 doubles in 1931?

47. Going into 1987, how many consecutive Gold Glove Awards had Ozzie Smith won?

103

The Infield—Questions

48. True or false? Frisch and Hornsby played on the same team.

49. Who played in more Cardinal games than any infielder?

50. Who holds the Cardinal record for most homers by a shortstop?

51. Name the only Cardinal to hit for the cycle twice.

52. What are the most home runs hit by a Cardinal switch-hitter in one season?

53. Name the only Card rookie to hit over 20 homers.

54. How many times did first baseman Ed Konetchy lead the club in doubles?

55. How many times did Konetchy lead the team in triples?

56. In what year did the regular Cardinal infield also become the All-Star infield?

57. What switch-hitting Cardinal infielder hit his first home run lefthanded after eight major league seasons?

58. Who played Rogers Hornsby in the movie *The Winning Team*?

The Infield—Questions

59. After playing in six seasons for the Cards, who hit 55 homers in the minors followed by a 56-homer season for the same minor league team?

60. Which three Cardinal second basemen drove in over 100 runs in a season?

61. Who was called "Pebbly Jack"?

62. What Cardinal third baseman made errors on three straight plays in a game blown by the Cards, 9-8, after an 8-0 lead?

63. What former Cardinal once hit 50 home runs in a season while striking out less than 50 times?

64. Name the only man to bat .400 and hit 40 homers in the same season.

65. What team did Hornsby and Bottomley finish their playing careers with?

66. What Cardinal shortstop was the first batter to face 15-year-old Joe Nuxhall?

67. Who had the lowest season batting average for any player in over 150 games?

68. What Cardinal second baseman batted six times in a game but had no official at-bats?

The Infield—Questions

69. What was Rogers Hornsby's best hit total for two consecutive seasons?

70. What Cardinal had two six-hit games?

71. What Card had 12 official times at bat in a doubleheader of two nine-inning games?

72. Name the only major league player to get eight doubles in two days.

73. What Cardinal hit three home runs in one game and did it again exactly one week later?

74. Whose season record for RBIs by a switch-hitter was broken by Mickey Mantle in 1956?

75. Who batted 639 times for the Cardinals in one season but hit no home runs?

76. Who had the lowest batting average of any non-pitcher to win the MVP Award?

77. Name the first infielder to wear eyeglasses.

78. Who was the youngest shortstop in modern baseball history to get 200 hits in one season?

79. How high a draft pick was MVP Keith Hernandez?

The Infield—Questions

80. What Cardinal second baseman still holds the record for most chances in one season?

81. How long has it been since an NL first baseman led the league in triples, and who did it?

82. When Tommy Herr had 110 RBIs in 1985, how many home runs did he hit?

83. Which Cardinal had the lowest season batting average of any shortstop?

84. Until 1987, who held the National League record for most homers in one season by a switch-hitter?

85. What Cardinal great had the same home run total in four consecutive seasons?

86. Before the Cardinals signed him, what team overlooked Tommy Herr in the draft?

Answers

1. Bill White got eight hits in a doubleheader and six more hits in a doubleheader the following day (July 17 and 18, 1961).

2. Ray Jablonski

3. Jim Bottomley, against Pittsburgh (May 7, 1925)

4. Terry Pendleton

5. Third baseman Les Bell hit .325.

6. Infielder Don Blasingame

7. 5'9" tall

The Infield—Answers

8. Joe Cunningham hit .345.

9. Shortstop Reuben Ewing

10. Charley Gelbert

11. Tommy Herr went from 49 RBIs to 110.

12. Andy High

13. Rogers Hornsby played for the 1926 Cardinals, 1927 Giants, 1928 Braves and 1929 Cubs.

14. Rogers Hornsby

15. Seven — six in a row as a Cardinal.

16. Julian Javier

17. Mike Jorgensen

18. Whitey Kurowski

19. Walter James Vincent Maranville

20. Rabbit Maranville

21. Card shortstop Marty Marion

22. Stolen bases (26)

23. Red Schoendienst (22-for-72, .306)

The Infield—Answers

24. Garry Templeton

25. Hits 230, RBIs 137, batting .363

26. Second baseman Mike Tyson

27. Twenty-five

28. Bill White

29. Ken Boyer

30. Tommy Herr fielded .992 in 1981.

31. Tommy Herr

32. 1980

33. Ozzie Smith

34. Frankie Frisch

35. Third base

36. Tommy Thevenow

37. Fielding percentage four times; putouts, assists and double plays twice each

38. Six

39. Ken Reitz

The Infield—Answers

40. Third baseman Jimmy Brown

41. Infielder Jimmy Brown

42. Marty Marion

43. Shortstop Marty Marion, second baseman Emil Verban and first baseman Ray Sanders

44. Frank Crespi

45. The Mets

46. Sparky Adams

47. Seven

48. True — in 1933 Hornsby returned to the Cardinals.

49. Red Schoendienst

50. Solly Hemus hit 15 in 1952.

51. Ken Boyer in 1961 and 1964

52. Ripper Collins hit 35 in 1934.

53. Ray Jablonski hit 21 in 1953.

54. Five

The Infield—Answers

55. Five

56. 1963 — White-1B, Javier-2B, Boyer-3B and Groat-ss

57. Ozzie Smith (in the NLCS against the Dodgers in 1985)

58. Frank Lovejoy

59. First baseman Steve Bilko

60. Hornsby, Frisch and Herr

61. Shortstop Jack Glasscock

62. Tommy Glaviano (1950)

63. Johnny Mize

64. Rogers Hornsby

65. The 1937 St. Louis Browns

66. George Fallon

67. Dal Maxvill hit .201 in 1970.

68. Miller Huggins walked four times and sacrificed twice.

69. Hornsby socked 485 base-hits from 1921 to 1922, a major league record for two consecutive seasons.

The Infield—Answers

70. Jim Bottomley (1924 and 1931)

71. Red Schoendienst

72. Red Schoendienst socked eight doubles in two days (single game June 5, doubleheader on June 6).

73. Johnny Mize on July 13 and July 20, 1938

74. Ripper Collins had 128 RBIs in 1934; Mickey Mantle had 130 RBIs in 1956.

75. Third baseman Milt Stock

76. Marty Marion batted .267 in 1944, his MVP year.

77. George "Specs" Torporcer

78. Garry Templeton (age 21)

79. Hernandez was picked on the 42d round of the June 1971 free-agent draft.

80. Frankie Frisch (1,059 chances in 1927)

81. 1946 — Stan Musial — 20 triples

82. Eight

83. George McBride batted .169 in 1906 (90 games).

The Infield—Answers

84.   Ripper Collins, 35

85.   Ken Boyer hit 24 homers in 1961, 1962, 1963 and 1964.

86.   All of them

The Outfield

1.   Which four Cardinal outfielders won Rookie of the Year Awards?

2.   In his ten-year career with the Cardinals, what was Ray Blades's best full-season batting average?

3.   Before Hornsby's time, what Hall-of-Fame outfielder batted .402 for the Cards?

4.   In what year did all three Cruz brothers play for the Cardinals?

5.   What Cardinal was so consistent that he had season averages of .336, .337, .338 and .339?

The Outfield—Questions

6.   What is Tito Landrum's given name?

7.   In 1982 what outfielder stole 68 bases in his first season as a Cardinal?

8.   What outfielder was acquired from the Red Sox and drove in 100 runs and batted .309 in his first season with the Cards (1974)?

9.   What was Enos Slaughter's nickname?

10.   What Hall-of-Fame outfielder scored exactly 100 runs for three straight seasons?

11.   What was Enos Slaughter's best season for doubles?

12.   Who posted the highest slugging average for a rookie?

13.   Within a five-year period, who was the only person to play on World Series winners with three different teams?

14.   What outfielder had a 29-game hitting streak in 1943?

15.   Who got ten straight hits during the 1929 season?

16.   Who smacked ten hits in a row during the 1936 season?

The Outfield — Questions

17. What Cardinal outfielder was traded after batting .237 and won the batting championship the next year with a .363 mark?

18. Who made the diving catch of Harvey Kuenn's line drive in the 1953 All-Star Game?

19. Who became the first major league player to steal 100 bases in his first two season?

20. What was unusual about Vince Coleman's first career home run?

21. Who recorded the highest single-season batting average for a National League switch-hitter?

22. In 1929 the Cardinals' regular outfielders all hit .325 or better. Name them.

23. Name the centerfielder who had the best season of his 14-year career with the 1944 Cards (.336).

24. When Musial batted .355 in 1951, who was the only other Cardinal regular to bat .300 that year?

25. How many runners did Enos Slaughter gun down from the outfield in 1939?

26. With Musial and Slaughter both in the service in 1945, who were the regular Cardinal outfielders?

The Outfield—Questions

27. What Cardinal outfielder led the National League in putouts and fielded 1.000 in 1966?

28. Who led all major league outfielders by throwing out 20 baserunners in 1979?

29. Who handled the incredible number of 566 chances in the Cardinal outfield in 1928?

30. What Cardinal outfielder was a former Hollywood stunt man and stand-in for Buster Keaton?

31. True or false? As a Cardinal, Lou Brock had over 3,000 hits.

32. How many times did Lou Brock reach the 200-hit mark and what was his best hit total?

33. Who was the first Cardinal to hit for the cycle?

34. What Cardinal missed a 700-at-bat season by only 11 at-bats?

35. Who holds the National League record for doubles in one season (64)?

36. In 1915 what Cardinal rookie led the league with 25 triples, more than half his lifetime total?

The Outfield—Questions

37. Whose 14 sacrifice flies brought his RBI total to over 100 in 1982?

38. Who batted 655 times and grounded into only two double plays?

39. When was the last time a Cardinal hit three homers in a game?

40. Who was the centerfielder on the 1957 Cardinals?

41. In Joe Medwick's first ten full seasons, what was his average number of hits?

42. Name the only Card to get 200 hits in a season and bat under .300.

43. With what team did Curt Flood start his big-league career?

44. With what team did Flood end his career?

45. With what team did Enos Slaughter finish his playing career?

46. Name the rookie outfielder who batted .373 for the 1930 Cards.

47. What outfielder played four years with the Cardinals with yearly hit totals of 146, 145, 143 and 146?

The Outfield—Questions

48.   Name the only National League player to get five hits in a game four times in one season.

49.   Who hit two pinch-hit grand slams for the Cardinals and one more for the Cubs?

50.   How many times did Lou Brock lead NL outfielders in errors?

51.   Who was the first batting champion to wear eyeglasses?

52.   Who handled 568 outfield chances from September 3, 1965, through June 4, 1967, without an error?

53.   In 1974 the entire Cardinal outfield batted over .300. Name them.

54.   What Cardinal outfielder had more triples than doubles in his five-year career?

55.   What Cardinal and ex-Giant hit the first home run in Candlestick Park, San Francisco (1960)?

Answers

1. Wally Moon (1954), Bill Virdon (1955),
    Bake McBride (1974) and Vince Coleman
    (1986)

2. Blades batted .342 in 1925.

3. Jesse Burkett

4. Hector, Jose and Tommy were on the
    Cards in 1973.

5. Chick Hafey

6. Terry Lee Landrum

7. Lonnie Smith

The Outfield—Answers

8. Reggie Smith

9. "Country"

10. Enos Slaughter

11. Slaughter socked a league-leading 52 doubles in 1939.

12. George Watkins slugged .621 in 1930.

13. Lonnie Smith was a member of the world champion Phillies (1980), Cardinals (1982) and Royals (1985)

14. Harry Walker

15. Chick Hafey

16. Joe Medwick

17. Harry "The Hat" Walker

18. Enos Slaughter

19. Vince Coleman

20. Coleman's first home run was an inside-the-park hit off Len Barker of the Braves. There was no play at the plate. It was Coleman's only homer of 1985.

21. Willie McGee hit .353 in 1985.

The Outfield—Answers

22. Ernie Orsatti .332 (rf), Chick Hafey .338 (lf), Taylor Douthit .336 (cf).

23. Johnny Hopp

24. Peanut Lowery (.303)

25. Eighteen

26. Red Schoendienst, left; Buster Adams, center; and Johnny Hopp, right

27. Curt Flood

28. George Hendrick

29. Taylor Douthit

30. Ernie Orsatti

31. False — Brock had 2,713 hits for St. Louis. His other hits were as a Cub.

32. Brock made 200 or more hits four times. His best was 206 in 1967.

33. Cliff Heathcote (July 13, 1918)

34. Lou Brock

35. Joe Medwick

36. Tommy Long

The Outfield—Answers

37. George Hendrick

38. Lou Brock

39. 1976 (Reggie Smith)

40. Ken Boyer

41. 196.7

42. Lou Brock hit .299 with 206 hits in 1967.

43. The Cincinnati Reds

44. The Washington Senators

45. Milwaukee Braves (1959)

46. George Watkins

47. George Watkins

48. Stan Musial (1948)

49. Outfielder Ron Northey

50. Seven (1964-1968, 1972 and 1973)

51. Chick Hafey

52. Curt Flood

53. Lou Brock, Reggie Smith and Bake McBride

The Outfield—Answers

54. Tommy Long had 49 triples and 47 doubles.

55. Leon Wagner

Managers and Coaches

1.   What managing milestone did Whitey Herzog achieve in 1987?

2.   Who said, "Oh, those bases on balls"?

3.   How many seasons did Red Schoendienst manage the Cardinals?

4.   Name the 30-year-old player/manager of the 1905 Cardinals.

5.   He played six years in the majors and managed five — all with the Cardinals. Name him.

6.   What teams did Frankie Frisch manage and how many pennants did he win?

Managers and Coaches—Questions

7.   Who said, "We could finish first or in an asylum"?

8.   What Cardinal shortstop and future manager led the National League in runs scored in 1952?

9.   What former Cardinal coach had a 1-2 pitching record for the Redbirds in 25 appearances spread out over five seasons?

10.   What former Cardinal player and current coach once broke up a ten-inning no-hitter with a home run?

11.   After Hornsby was traded in December 1926, who took over as Cardinal manager?

12.   What former Cardinal player and coach once hit a home run that won a pennant?

13.   What Cardinal coach played in four decades (1939-1960) and won two American League batting crowns?

14.   What Cardinal coaches were brothers and also batting champs?

15.   Who was known as "The Duke of Tralee"?

Managers and Coaches—Questions

16. Between 1925 and 1939, who managed three different National League teams to pennants?

17. What major league teams did Whitey Herzog play for?

18. What Cardinal coach was a basketball star at Duquesne University?

19. What is Whitey Herzog's uniform number?

20. What former Cardinal coaches were the first two National League players to hit grand-slam homers in the World Series?

21. When Hornsby took over as Cardinal manager in mid-1925, whom did he replace?

22. Name the first Cardinal manager to win two pennants in a row.

23. Name the first Card manager to win three pennants in a row.

24. The Cardinals had one manager per year from 1950 to 1952. Name the three managers.

25. Who replaced Vern Rapp as Cardinal manager until Ken Boyer took over?

Managers and Coaches—Questions

26. In 1980 the Cardinals had four managers. Name them.

27. What managers did the Cardinals let go after they won pennants?

28. Who managed the Cardinals for part of 1980 and had 1,980 hits while a player for the Cards?

29. Who became a player/manager for the Cards when traded by the Giants?

30. Who became a player/manager for the Cards when traded by the Phils?

31. Who was the last manager of the St. Louis Browns?

32. What manager was nicknamed "Deacon"?

33. What was Miller Huggins's nickname?

34. Who was the only Cardinal manager in the twentieth century to win four pennants and not make the Hall of Fame?

35. What former Cardinal coach pitched professionally in six decades?

36. Who was a Cardinal coach for 13 straight years?

132

Managers and Coaches—Questions

37. Name the first switch-hitter elected to the Hall of Fame.

38. What were Eddie Stanky's nicknames?

39. What Cardinal player and manager played in the World Series with three different teams within five years?

40. What Cardinal manager once made second team All-American in college football?

41. Who was the first-base coach for the Cardinals at the time Brock broke Cobb's lifetime stolen-base record?

Answers

1. Herzog won his 1,000th game.

2. Frankie Frisch

3. Thirteen

4. Jimmy Burke

5. Eddie Dyer

6. Frisch managed the Cards (1933-1938), the Pirates (1940-1946) and the Cubs (1949-1951). His only pennant came in 1934.

7. Cards manager Frankie Frisch (1936)

Managers and Coaches—Answers

8. Solly Hemus

9. Tony Kaufmann

10. Johnny Lewis

11. Catcher Bob O'Farrell

12. Dick Sisler (1950) as a Phillie

13. Mickey Vernon

14. Dixie and Harry Walker

15. Cardinal catcher and manager Roger Bresnahan

16. Bill McKechnie managed the Pirates, Cards and Reds to NL championships.

17. Washington, Kansas City, Baltimore and Detroit

18. Dave Ricketts

19. Twenty-four

20. Chuck Hiller (1962 Giants) and Ken Boyer (1964 Cards)

21. Branch Rickey

22. Gabby Street (1930, 1931)

Managers and Coaches—Answers

23. Billy Southworth (1942, 1943, 1944)

24. Eddie Dyer (1950), Marty Marion (1951)
    and Eddie Stanky (1952)

25. Jack Krol

26. Ken Boyer (18-33), Jack Krol (0-1),
    Whitey Herzog (38-35) and Red Schoen-
    dienst (18-19)

27. Rogers Hornsby was traded after the 1926
    season; Bill McKechnie was fired after the
    1928 campaign; Johnny Keane quit after
    winning in 1964.

28. Red Schoendienst

29. Eddie Stanky

30. Solly Hemus

31. Marty Marion (1953)

32. Bill McKechnie

33. "The Mighty Mite"

34. Billy Southworth won pennants for the
    Cards in 1942, 1943 and 1944, and for
    the Braves in 1948.

35. Hub Kittle

Managers and Coaches—Answers

36. Mike Gonzalez

37. Frankie Frisch

38. "The Brat" and "Muggsy"

39. Eddie Stanky played in the World Series with the 1947 Dodgers, the 1948 Braves and the 1951 Giants.

40. Frankie Frisch

41. Sonny Ruberto

Miscellaneous

1. What pitcher was the first to throw a no-hitter against the Cardinals in the twentieth century?

2. True or false? Stan Musial holds the Cardinals' consecutive-game hitting-streak record?

3. Who won the Most Valuable Player Award in the year Rogers Hornsby batted .424?

4. Who had more total bases (450) in one season than any player in the National League history?

5. What much-travelled outfielder got his 999th and final hit as a Cardinal?

Miscellaneous—Questions

6.   Where was John Tudor when he broke his leg in 1987?

7.   How many homers did Ken and Clete Boyer hit between them?

8.   What three Cardinal MVPs later played for the Mets?

9.   Who was known as "Sunny Jim"?

10. Who batted only once in his career and made the Hall of Fame?

11. What pitcher lost 19 straight games after he left the Cards?

12. What pitcher lost 18 straight games before coming to the Cards?

13. Who pitched in a total of 24 games for the Phillies, Orioles, Cards and Astros and wound up with a 0-0 lifetime record?

14. What have Mike Torrez and Rick Wise done that only three others have accomplished?

15. The Cards had two Blaylocks on the 1959 club. Give their first names.

16. True or false? All three Boyer brothers were in the major leagues together.

140

Miscellaneous—Questions

17. What state did the three Boyer brothers hail from?

18. What state did Mort and Walker Cooper come from?

19. Three one-time Cardinal pitchers had 20-years careers with less than 200 wins lifetime and no 20-game-winning seasons. Name them.

20. True or false? Lou Brock spent his entire career with the Cardinals.

21. What fifties MVP pitched for the Pirates, Houston, the Cubs, Phillies and the Cardinals, after winning 99 games in the American League?

22. What Cardinal relief pitcher wrote several good books on baseball?

23. How old was Pepper Martin when he pinch-ran for Tulsa in a Texas League game?

24. What Cardinal great was born on February 29?

25. Who was known as "The Wild Hoss of the Osage"?

26. Who was nicknamed "The Crab"?

Miscellaneous—Questions

27. Who was destined to play at least one full season with the Cardinals?

28. Who was called "The Baby Bull"?

29. Who was known as "Cha-Cha"?

30. Who held the lifetime record for home runs before Babe Ruth?

31. Which one of the five Delahanty brothers spent his entire major league career with the Cardinals?

32. Who batted 17 times for the Cards in 1953 and retired with a lifetime batting average of .353?

33. Who was known as "The Lip"?

34. Who managed in the major leagues in the 1930s and the 1970s?

35. What former Cardinal reserve had his greatest season as an American Leaguer in 1959 — the same year his son, a future major leaguer, was born?

36. What Hall-of-Famer was a boyhood chum of Joe Garagiola?

37. Describe Lou Brock's most famous home run.

142

Miscellaneous—Questions

38. Who said, "So many guys come and go here, if we win the pennant our shares would be 50 dollars apiece"?

39. Who said, "There are so many new faces around here, I thought I'd been traded"?

40. Name the Cards Hall-of-Famer called "Pop."

41. Who was known as "The Mad Hungarian"?

42. Who was called "Hug" for short?

43. Name two Redbirds whose last names begin with the letter I.

44. What current major league manager is the son of a Cardinal who pitched for the club from 1938 to 1951?

45. What former Cardinal pitcher threw the pitch (as a Giant) that enabled Willie Mays to make that great World Series catch?

46. What 13-year veteran outfielder and utility infielder had his only .300 season as a Cardinal in 1951?

47. For nine major league seasons, what name did Leopold Christopher Hoernschemeyer play under?

143

Miscellaneous—Questions

48. What is Bake McBride's real name?

49. What were Joe Medwick's two nick-names?

50. Who was a teammate of Stan Musial, Willie Mays and Sandy Koufax?

51. Who had a 200-hit, 100-RBI, .350-average season in 1921, and died after the following season?

52. Who was "Little Napoleon"?

53. Who played every position except pitcher and batted .339 for the 1894 Cards?

54. Where was Minnie Minoso born?

55. What was Johnny Mize's famous nickname?

56. Who was pitcher Wilmer Mizell known as?

57. In 1923 what Cardinal reserve outfielder batted .343 while his brother was batting .306 for Pittsburgh? Thirty-one years later (1954), his nephew batted .342 for the Giants.

58. Where were the four O'Neill brothers from?

Miscellaneous—Questions

59. What teammate of Stan Musial attended Notre Dame with Stan's son?

60. Who was "The Arkansas Hummingbird"?

61. Who was nicknamed "The Hat"?

62. What Cardinals spelled their names the same way backwards?

63. What is the longest hitting streak of Jack Clark's career?

64. What AL Hall-of-Famer hit the line drive that broke Dizzy Dean's toe in the 1937 All-Star Game?

65. How did the Cardinals acquire John Tudor?

66. Who never won an MVP Award, but came in second twice and third once?

67. In the thirties, what was the name of the Cards' hillbilly band?

68. What five Cardinals reached over 3,000 total bases (as Cardinals)?

69. What Cardinals combined to lead the league in total bases for seven years in a row (1934 to 1940)?

145

Miscellaneous—Questions

70. In 1987 who was inducted into the broad-caster's wing of baseball's Hall of Fame?

71. Who broadcasted Cardinal games for 16 years and played for the Cards for nine years?

72. What opposing team drew the biggest crowd at the new Busch Stadium?

73. In 1982 what team did the Cards beat on opening day (on the road) by a 14-3 score?

74. How many All-Star Games did Stan Musial appear in?

75. In 1960 who pinch hit successfully in both All-Star Games?

76. Who was the only National League player to win MVP Awards at two different positions?

77. Who played one year with the Cardinals and was killed in a plane crash?

78. Prior to playing for the Cardinals, who was the only player to be named MVP in both the International League (1970) and the American Association (1976)?

79. Who did the Cards give up to get Curt Davis, Clyde Shoun, Tuck Stainback and $185,000?

Miscellaneous—Questions

80. Name the only two Cardinals with the 1987 team who were on the roster when Whitey Herzog took over as Cardinal manager in 1980.

81. The Cardinals have won more MVP Awards than any National League team. How many?

82. In 1924 what 26-year-old Cardinal rookie had a two-year-old brother who would make the majors 30 years later?

83. What are the most and fewest runs scored by a Cardinal team in one season?

84. Name five Cardinal players that were All-Stars in both leagues.

85. Who gave up Ernie Banks's record fifth grand slam of the 1955 season?

86. What Hall-of-Famer gave up Lou Brock's first major league hit?

87. Off whom did Lou Brock hit his homer into the centerfield bleachers of the Polo Grounds in 1962?

88. Whose potential no-hitters were ruined twice by a Lou Brock hit?

89. Who became only the second youngest pitcher in modern history to win games

Miscellaneous—Questions

in both the National and American Leagues (age 22)?

90. In 1984 what Cardinal pitcher hit home runs batting right- and left-handed?

91. Since 1901, how many times have the Cardinals led the NL in home runs?

92. What Cardinal catcher had a stadium named after him?

93. Name the Cardinal pitcher who surrendered the first home run ever hit in Montreal's Jarry Park.

94. In 1968 what pitcher was the winner in eight extra-inning games?

95. What one-season Cardinal pitching record has Stoney McGlynn held for 80 years?

96. What is the correct first name of Bruce Sutter?

97. Which three members of the 1963 Cardinals became announcers for major league clubs?

98. Joe Hoerner pitched in 493 games with seven different clubs. How many games did he start?

Miscellaneous—Questions

99.   Where was Moe Drabowsky born?

Answers

1. Christy Mathewson (1901)

2. False — Rogers Hornsby hit safely in 33 straight games in 1922.

3. Brooklyn pitcher Dazzy Vance (1924)

4. Rogers Hornsby (1922)

5. Tommie Agee

6. In the Cardinals dugout

7. 444 — Ken hit 282; Clete hit 162.

8. Ken Boyer, Joe Torre and Keith Hernandez

Miscellaneous—Answers

9. Hall-of-Famer Jim Bottomley

10. Walter Alston

11. Craig Anderson

12. Roger Craig

13. John Anderson

14. Torrez and Wise have beaten all 26 current major league teams.

15. Bob and Gary

16. True — in 1955 pitcher Cloyd Boyer finished his career with Kansas City. Ken (St. Louis) and Clete (K.C.) came up the same year.

17. Missouri

18. Missouri

19. Lindy McDaniel, Curt Simmons and Hoyt Wilhelm

20. False — Brock started with the 1961 Cubs and came to the Cards June 15, 1964.

21. Bobby Shantz

22. Jim Brosnan

Miscellaneous—Answers

23. Fifty-four years old (1958)

24. Pepper Martin

25. Pepper Martin

26. Jesse Burkett (Hall-of-Famer)

27. Jose Cardenal

28. Orlando Cepeda

29. Orlando Cepeda

30. Roger Connor

31. Joe Delahanty

32. Grant Dunlap

33. Leo Durocher

34. Leo Durocher

35. Tito Francona

36. Yogi Berra

37. Brock was only the second player to homer into the Polo Grounds' centerfield bleachers (as a Cub).

38. Cards infielder Danny Cater (1975)

Miscellaneous—Answers

39. Ken Oberkfell, in spring training 1981

40. Jesse "Pop" Haines

41. Pitcher Al Hrabosky

42. Miller Huggins

43. Dane Iorg and Walt Irwin

44. Astros manager Hal Lanier is the son of Max Lanier who pitched for the Cardinals for 12 years.

45. Don Liddle

46. Harry "Peanuts' Lowery

47. Lee Magee

48. Arnold Ray McBride

49. "Ducky" and "Muscles"

50. Pitcher Bob Miller

51. Austin McHenry

52. John McGraw — the Hall-of-Fame manager played one season with the Cardinals.

53. Doggie Miller

Miscellaneous—Answers

54. Havana Cuba (November 29, 1922)

55. "The Big Cat"

56. "Vinegar Bend" Mizell

57. Heinie Mueller

58. Cardinals Jack and Mike O'Neill were born in Ireland; non-Cards Jim and Steve were born in Pennsylvania.

59. Mike Shannon

60. Cardinal pitcher and later umpire Lon Warneke

61. Harry Walker

62. Third baseman KAZAK (Eddie) and catcher SALAS (Mark).

63. Clark batted safely in 26 consecutive games in 1978 as a Giant.

64. Earl Averill

65. The Cards traded outfielder George Hendrick and catcher Steve Barnard to the Pirates for Tudor and outfielder Brian Harper.

66. Johnny Mize

Miscellaneous—Answers

67. "The Mississippi Mudcats"

68. Musial, Brock, Hornsby, Slaughter and Boyer

69. Ripper Collins (1934), Joe Medwick (1935-1937) and Johnny Mize (1938-1940).

70. Jack Buck

71. Mike Shannon

72. The New York Mets (50,548)

73. The Houston Astros

74. Twenty-four

75. Stan Musial

76. Stan Musial won two MVP Awards as an outfielder (1943, 1948), and one as a first baseman (1946).

77. Charlie Peete

78. Roger Freed

79. Dizzy Dean

80. Bob Forsch and Tommy Herr

Miscellaneous—Answers

81. Seventeen, going back to Hornsby (1925)

82. Jesse Fowler, brother of Art Fowler

83. Most — 1,004 in 1930; fewest — 372 in 1908 (both NL records)

84. Richie Allen, George Hendrick, Johnny Mize, Ted Simmons and Reggie Smith

85. Lindy McDaniel

86. Robin Roberts

87. Al Jackson of the Mets

88. Jim Barr (1973, 1975)

89. Dave LaPoint

90. Joaquin Andujar

91. Only five

92. Tim McCarver

93. Nelson Briles

94. Joe Hoerner

95. Most innings pitched — 352.1

96. Howard

Miscellaneous—Answers

97.   Tim McCarver, Mike Shannon and Bill White

98.   None

99.   In Poland